Fly the Phoenix

FLY THE PHOENIX

Inspired by 'The Art of Creativity'

Lizzie Davies

ARCOBALENO

Copyright © Lizzie Davies 2021
First published in 2021 by ARCOBALENO
Catharine Place, Bath, BA1 2PS

Distributed by Gardners Books, 1 Whittle Drive, Eastbourne, East Sussex, BN23 6QH
Tel: +44(0)1323 521555 | Fax: +44(0)1323 521666

The right of Lizzie Davies to be identified as the author of the work has been asserted herein in accordance with the Copyright, Designs and Patents Act 1988.

All rights reserved. This book is sold subject to the condition that it shall not, by way of trade or otherwise, be lent, resold, hired out or otherwise circulated without the publisher's prior consent in any form of binding or cover other than that in which it is published and without a similar condition including this condition being imposed on the subsequent purchaser.

British Library Cataloguing in Publication Data
A catalogue record for this book is available from
the British Library

ISBN 978-1-8382695-0-0

Typeset by Amolibros, Milverton, Somerset
www.amolibros.com
This book production has been managed by Amolibros
Printed and bound by the Lavenham Press, Lavenham, Suffolk, UK

© Candala of Rebirth by Lizzie Davies
Photograph by Peter J. Stone

A Candala is an illuminated artform designed to light up our world. Built as an installation with positive intent, it is based on the circle and incorporates light and symbolic materials.

Contents

A Guiding Light for our Times — vii
Acknowledgments — xii
A Few Words of Explanation — xiii
Introduction — xvii

Part One — 1
'The Art of Creativity'
Verses & Reflections — 2

Part Two — 31
The Ascent of the Phoenix

The Intention — 32
The Vision — 32
The Invitation — 33
Purpose — 33
Aims — 33
Mantra — 34
The Ten-point Call to Action — 35
What To Do Next — 39

To the creative spirit —
that spark of love, light and compassion within

A Guiding Light for our Times

"Be creative as God is creative. There are two ways we can live our life: mechanical and creative. We are manifested in the image and likeness of God – that is to live a creative life. But we also have a tendency to fall into mechanical life. It is a kind of spiritual death. When our energy is flowing out, in interacting with others, we may feel a sense of fulfilment but when it stops due to situations like Lockdown we may fall into depression, a kind of death. Lizzie Davies, in her book, *Fly the Phoenix*, wonderfully shows the nature of creative living and the means by which one can enter into a creative life. I myself have benefitted from reading this work and I am sure it will help all those who wish to understand what living is and how to live creatively. I congratulate Lizzie Davies for her compassion in sharing her insights, which she has discovered in the difficult situations of her life."

Br. John Martin Sahajananda OSB (Order of Saint Benedict),
Shantivanam, Tamilnadu, South India.
Author of several books including *You are the Light*

"Just as the Phoenix regenerates itself, so Lizzie Davies arises from her own ashes through the challenges of Lockdown 2020. You too might have had your own challenges. Her deep listening ignited a response from her soul enabling her to rebirth herself. This illuminating, deeply engaging handbook demonstrates how we have an innate ability as humans to marry the love in our hearts with our minds to engage with our passion for life. Through her methodology, she shows us the great secrets to a new way, a new world, right now in response to our global crisis. Lizzie invites us to live creatively and rise like the Phoenix. Great advice for us all!"

Rev. Hilary Franklin
One Spirit Interfaith Minister & Voice work Facilitator, Devizes, Wiltshire, UK

"Lizzie Davies' invitation to fly the Phoenix takes us both inward into our own being, and then out into the world. With great lightness of touch, she invites us to find our own special brand of creativity; and that comes from a spacious part of ourselves where love and inspiration dwell. She speaks of the planetary emergency linked with our shocking behaviour, calling for more reverence for what is true. Then, when we dare to listen to the call of our souls, the guiding light within will show the way. Where does each one of us find joy? As we rise like the Phoenix, what makes our hearts sing?"

Hazel Marshall
Counsellor & Psychotherapist
Founder & Director the Transpersonal Centre, Rock Bank, Leicestershire, UK

"*Fly the Phoenix* is a short and motivating read for anyone called to connect to their creativity. It is a powerful affirmation that we don't have to *do* anything to be creative, but simply allow our natural power to run through us. It is always inspiring to read how connecting to their inner artist has changed someone's life, and, to us at Create Space, this short book has simply confirmed the understanding that what the world needs right now is more intuitive artistic focus."

Nicolene Burger
Co-Creator at Create Space Guided Art, Cape Town, South Africa

Lizzie Davies
Creative & Transformational Guide

Lizzie Davies is a writer, performance poet, Candala artist and peace activist. During Covid Lockdown, she survived an agonising trial by fire alone which prompted her to ask the question, 'How can I use my creativity to serve others in these troubled times?'

Schooled in resilience and reinvention, Lizzie wrote this book and re-branded her various initiatives under the auspices of *Fly the Phoenix*. The title conveys her hard-won philosophy that we can rise above our limitations and receive our flying colours if we turn within, are true to ourselves and do the work.

Lizzie has a broad wingspan of life experience. She is passionate about sharing her creativity and innovative method of transformation, Phoenix Wisdom. She is committed to building an international Phoenix community and lives in Bath, UK.

www.flythephoenix.co.uk

Acknowledgements

My abundant, heartfelt thanks go to all the people and services who helped to pull me through my Covid Lockdown ordeal, including the network of prayerful support from individuals and the prayer list at Christ Church, Bath.

In particular I would like to thank 'Ulster woman extraordinaire', Clare Whelan, and my next door neighbours, Di & Andrew for their generous care and support throughout. I also wish to thank my friends for helping to keep me going at various times: Christine, Sue Caden, Guy Douglas, Graham Fitch, Orlando Murrin, Anna Keith, Daphne Radenhurst, Shirlie Roden, Thandi Lubimbi, Bren and Mal Wall and Roger Whelan. Also Wiltshire Mental Health Partnership NHS Trust, The Samaritans Helpline, The Trauma & Orthopaedic Department & Rheumatology Department at the RUH (Royal United Hospital), the physio and occupational therapists, Age UK Bath & North East Somerset: David Seymour (Befriender), Judith Boby (cleaner) and Steve Best (IT support).

In addition I would like to thank warmly all those who helped in getting this book out there, my 'sounding boards' Bren, Daphne, Shirl, Sue, Helen Cain, Jude Hammond and Ros Floyd Sanchez, my editor Christine Whaite, Oluwatosin Onile-Ere Rotimi, Dr. Chris Stephens, Director of The Holburne Museum in Bath and Jane Tatam of Amolibros who helped to put this book together.

A Few Words of Explanation

Page 6
The term I AM can be interpreted as the metaphysical name of the spiritual self as distinguished from the human self, or the name of God. What we call this Higher Power depends on cultural, religious and psycho-spiritual understanding. Here are a few names that you may be familiar with: The Source, The Beloved, Great Spirit, The Cosmos, The Universe, Higher Self.

Page 28
Tao is a Chinese word signifying the 'way', 'path', 'route', 'road'. In the context of East Asian religions and East Asian philosophy, the Tao is the natural order of the universe of which we are a part. This intuitive knowing of 'life' cannot be grasped as a concept; it is known through actual living experience of one's everyday being.

Page 37
The Global Circle of Peace is a new way of uniting the people of the world through a creative movement for universal peace. Their website offers Peace PAX, which is a resource pack of creative material to cultivate inner and outer peace. Dedicated to our children and our children's children, it is designed for personal and family use and includes ideas for schools and community

groups. It can be used daily, weekly, monthly and to mark significant occasions and global events. www.theglobalcircleofpeace.com

The words of 'The Circle of Peace Dedication' are taken from 'Time for Peace on Earth', a mime-poem by Lizzie Davies created for *Time for Peace* – an interactive arts project. The piece was first performed at the *Time for Peace* tree-planting ceremony at Prinknash Abbey, Gloucestershire on 18th March 1998 when a rowan was planted. The rowan tree has a long, sacred history. Since ancient times, people have been planting a rowan beside their home, as in Celtic mythology it's known as the 'Tree of Life' and symbolises courage, wisdom and protection.

"I used to think the top environmental problems were biodiversity loss, ecosystem collapse and climate change. I thought that with 30 years of good science we could address those problems. But I was wrong. The top environmental problems are selfishness, greed and apathy…and to deal with those we need a spiritual and cultural transformation…and we scientists don't know how to do that."

— *James Gustave Speth*

Introduction

We live in challenging times when our souls, our society and our planet hang perilously in the balance. Our global crises are calling us to emulate the Phoenix, a mythical bird widely known as a universal symbol of regeneration, with the capacity to be reborn from the ashes of its own death.

The idea for this book emerged from my Covid lockdown experience. Whilst I did not suffer by catching the Covid virus, I did go through a veritable trial by fire. Over a period of three months of living alone, I became seriously ill and incapacitated and eventually made my peace with the possibility of dying alone.

Fly the Phoenix offers inspiration for reflection, transformation and action. Part I of this book offers a profound, yet accessible, teaching on creativity with Reflections on its relevance for today. The initial inspiration was 'downloaded' in 2000 as a succinct, stand-alone poem to encapsulate a broad understanding of creativity. The teaching has been the bedrock of my inner enquiry and spiritual practice ever since, helping to reshape my perception, thinking and behaviour.

My intention in sharing 'The Art of Creativity' now is that it may be of enduring benefit to your reflective path of self-discovery. The teaching underpins the vision for The Ascent of the Phoenix, a creative, interactive project in Part II, the purpose of which is to inspire personal and collective transformation.

Creativity has been my saving grace. Having survived major trauma, I can testify to the wonder, mystery and restorative power of the creative spirit that continues to inform my ongoing healing, transformation and creative practice.

May *Fly the Phoenix* provide an uplifting, useful resource as you recover from Covid Lockdown and face the future. As one who has struggled, I pray that it will touch the minds and hearts of anyone who has felt, or continues to feel, isolated, lonely and grief-stricken. You are not alone.

I invite you to *fly the Phoenix* whose time, I believe, has come.

Bath, Somerset
Autumn 2020

Part One

'The Art of Creativity'

I

The art of creativity is our innate ability
To express at any one time
Our highest aspiration and deepest truth
A cross 'twixt the human and sublime
Ever present in us all is a power we can call upon
Whenever we are yearning to be free
By embodying inspiration
We can access liberation
Through The Source – Creativity

In the midst of our Covid and planetary crises, we need to become creative about reshaping our inner as well as our outer lives. By connecting to our highest aspiration and digging deep inside ourselves, we can tap into our inner resources. This enables us to become more self-sustainable so we can lead a more simple, balanced and harmonious life.

Creativity can be life-enhancing and deeply satisfying – all part of increasing our mental, emotional and spiritual health and well-being. Whether at home in the kitchen, at school, at work or at the highest level of scientific and artistic innovation, we can all play our part. Play is good for the soul and fertile ground for invention.

Inspiration is free and accessible to all if we are open to it. It is a question of how we perceive and embody its presence.

II

The creative spirit is ingenious
In a flash things can change for evermore
A spark might strike in the dead of night
Or when we don't focus on the problem anymore
Something can click through spontaneous laughter
Lateral thinking or innocent play
The flames often take when the heat's beneath our feet
When we get ourselves out of the way

Often, in our darkest hour, when we feel we can no longer endure a problem, a portal of possibility is opened and we come to see the light at the end of the tunnel.

Imagination is a powerful tool for transformation and can lift our mood when we are feeling low. If you are struggling with a problem, try lighting a candle and focus your attention on the flame. This can be extremely comforting. Equally, you could close your eyes and imagine that light at the end of tunnel coming to meet you just where you are.

Most of us have had moments when a bright idea has come to us out of the blue. Relaxation is vital if we are to open ourselves to new ideas and our inner gold mine of creativity. Becoming totally absorbed in a sense of play, a hobby or your creative or spiritual practice, such as meditation or mindfulness can help you switch off. Some people work well under pressure, but take care to balance this with dedicated downtime too.

Discovering our own creativity, perhaps for the first time, can be our saving grace and raise our spirits when we are suffering or feeling lost.

Laughter is one of the best medicines and is now recognised for its short and long-term health benefits of dealing with stress. It is also fun and immensely liberating to laugh at ourselves and not take ourselves too seriously.

III

The power to enthuse is oft bestowed by The Muse
When we are aligned to a stillness of mind
When we're anchored and centred in our bodies
A quiet place is cleared for us to find
Beyond the 'little me' lies our true identity
The seed of the great I AM
Which loves to manifest when we stop to take a rest
From the crazy busy business log-jam

Our frenzied, fractured society is hungry for soul food. What we identify with defines us. We have only to look at our insane, narcissistic 'Me, Me, Me' culture of Selfies, and obsession with Celebrity status and Reality TV Shows to see that we have lost our way. This egomania is the very antithesis of our hope for a better, brighter and more sustainable world.

Slowing down, learning to still the mind, being quiet, and centred in our bodies are some of the greatest gifts we can give to ourselves and the people around us. It may be a lifelong practice, but all the more reason to start now and be part of a sane, cultural revolution.

Being real, reconnecting to something greater than ourselves, is surely an enriching and rewarding path to follow, because it has meaning, depth and satisfies our soul's inner yearning.

IV

The art of creativity is sacred unity
Borne of the male and female within
Through the marriage of our innermost Love-Wisdom
We deepen our connection to our kin
If we want to build a sense of community
And find meaning in a real place
We must counter our obsession with the outer
Through the exploration of inner space

We need a healthy balance between our feminine and masculine nature if we are to manifest our true self and save ourselves, our society and our planet.

Covid brought the world to a stop, almost overnight. Many people who were furloughed, and those shielding, were able to taste the benefits of that space and time to reflect. Some reported reconnecting to a softer, more vulnerable side of themselves where they felt more keenly their own suffering and that of others.

Making room in our mind and our heart, whether for creativity, our loved ones, or for people for whom we feel empathy, takes vigilance. Love and compassion need inner space to grow and take root in the garden of our soul.

Inner and outer decluttering is essential if we are to make space for new ideas and see the world afresh.

V

Cultivating stillness is a contemplative art
Engendering the culture of The Whole of which we're part
In listening to ourselves we get in touch with who we are
The lost aspects of our nature are collected from afar
In slowing down our pace we're more willing to embrace
The unknown and put ourselves to one side
Which signals the move to get into the groove
Of our intuition – our teacher and guide

Developing our intuition is a smart move. It is one of our most important resources and we ignore it at our peril. In terms of creative practice, we need to listen to and trust our quiet, inner promptings and follow the creative impulse as it moves through us without impeding its flow. The unconscious mind has a life of its own and can bring forth treasures from the depths.

How can we restore balance to our obsession with outer image and addiction to materialistic acquisition? Reflection, contemplation, meditation and mindfulness are all tools of the inner life. These practices can help us gain insights into those parts of ourselves that we need to retrieve and with which we need to reconnect.

We are all living with a sense of the unknown as we move through Covid and beyond. Making friends with 'not knowing' takes practice, yet it is all part of learning to live in the moment. 'Not knowing' is a brilliant place to be to activate creativity. Make the blank page or the blank canvas your friend. Celebrate the emptiness and space and step into the shoes of your inner Zen monk or nun.

VI

Silence is to sound
What space is to form
When we gain our perfect poise
We can move beyond the norm
Accessing dimensions hidden to our outer eye and ear
Through lighting up our consciousness a new world can appear
Miracles happen, synchronicities abound
As we refine our awareness of the vibration of sound

Developing our inner resources in times of personal crisis and at this time of global change is an investment worth making.

Silence is golden. If we talked less and stopped filling the space with all 'the stuff' we think we know, then it would afford us the space to tune in to inner wisdom and illuminating guidance. The soul yearns to be heard. It is so important to listen to ourselves and each other. By turning within, we can hone our sensitivity to think new thoughts, ideas and work to enrich ourselves, our loved ones and our community.

Our perception is an ever-changing kaleidoscope. We never know when the lights will go on and we will see with new eyes or hear with new ears. Refining our awareness through regular creative practice and spiritual disciplines like meditation, mindfulness, T'ai chi or Qigong can help us become more fine-tuned and connect us to a sense of inner acceptance and peace, especially during the most challenging times.

To become an integrated, rounded human being and a creative instrument takes serious dedication. Cultivating a balanced, healthy interconnection between our body-mind-spirit is all part of this dynamic process.

VII

The art of creativity is pure receptivity
Through the bridge of our body-mind
We are attuned to become living instruments
Contributing our gifts to humankind
To access our inner voice is an in-the-moment choice
A daily practice through our presence of mind
To be or not to be? To see or not to see?
To do or not to do? … Pretend we're blind?

We are all potential 'receivers'. Some easily pick up inspirational cues and non-verbal signals from people, others are oblivious to the information that is under their nose. Such is the human spectrum of multi-sensory awareness and our ability to read and interpret subtle energy. If you want to become open to receiving inspiration and inner guidance, take time to develop your visual, auditory and kinetic senses.

We all want to be received by our loved ones and that requires 'the other' making time and space, to listen, hear and understand. In a culture that is hell-bent on 'doing', remember the art of being, which puts us in touch with a spacious part of ourselves where love and inspiration dwell.

Being present is the key to life. This is a great challenge for us all, especially in times of threat, and the unknown, when we tend to cling to the past or escape to the future. It is never too late to start turning our life around. If you truly want to find yourself and the answers to life, you will be shown the way.

Global warming and our planetary emergency have revealed the stark consequences of our shocking behaviour, showing us just how blind, cut-off and irreverent we have become. We can reverse our egomania if we put our minds to it, but first perhaps we have to surrender our personal selfishness, greed, and apathy.

VIII

Why did we break The Circle?
Life doesn't live in straight lines
Through cutting our bond with Nature
We've stopped seeing the Wonders and Signs
Whatever the manifold reasons
Now is the time to reconnect
To Life in all of its seasons
Humanity is ours to resurrect

Let's develop the power of our heart to the depth of the power of our mind.
Let's become supremely human and make the world infinitely kind.

IX

Creativity follows the circle of life
According to universal law
In our cycles, rhythms and patterns
Lie the keys to our sacred door
Through circulating energy
Time and time again
There's always the chance to step into the dance
Whatever our past or our pain

Creativity like life, turns in cycles. Become aware of the right time to sow seeds, reap the harvest and allow a field of endeavour or relationship to remain fallow.

Pushing against the natural rhythm of life causes imbalance and alienation from ourselves and each other. When we get out of our head and tune into our body, our felt sense and our gut instinct, we reconnect to the flow of life. Being grounded, with our feet firmly planted on the earth, reconnects us to the natural world.

The present moment and the breath are natural resources freely available at any time. The dance of life is always calling us home.

X

The art of creativity is the focus of acuity
A laser that can cut to the core
Insight with rigour and mindfulness
And a compassionate intent to restore
Can enable the light of discernment
To lift the veil from our eyes
So we find the courage to live our truth
And sever our negative ties

A sharp, incisive mind and business acumen both have a role to play in cutting through the dross and asking penetrating questions. Yet this hard, masculine part of our nature needs to be balanced by our softer, feminine side, which can be compassionate and accommodating of our failures and shortcomings as a part of self-enquiry and growth.

Cultivating both male and female sides of our nature is all a part of the richness of life's learning. If we are to help ourselves grow and be of service to others, it is important to become adept at using both the creative side and analytic side of our brain. Discernment is vital if we are to sort the wheat from the chaff.

The marriage of our head and our heart, plus a sincere intention to see the error of our ways, can lead to a breakthrough that can be life-changing. Severing negative ties and attachments, whether to a habit, a relationship or a piece of creative work, requires courage. When we let go for the right reason, in the right way at the right time, there is a sense of relief and a sense of moving beyond self-imposed limitations.

XI

The ultimate experiment is ours to manifest
If we face our greatest demons and take on board the test
We have to die to be reborn all the time in little ways
So the patterns of the past are not repeated all our days
If our spirit is to fly we must pass through gates of death
Rising as the Phoenix with every single breath
By surrendering our little selves on to the sacred fire
Our soul is reignited by the One creative fire

Facing our demons is no longer just an individual, private affair. Confronted with our planetary emergency and the mirror of our collective thinking, habits and behaviour, this is very much a shared problem. I am society. Everyone is. What we think, say and do each day shapes and influences the world around us.

If we do not want history to repeat itself, whether within our own family, our community, our nation or our world, then changing our personal mindset and behaviour is key. We can create afresh and build a better, brighter future.

Our creative fire, our indomitable creative spirit, is one of the most powerful resources in the world. Now is the time for us to meet our trial by fire with creative fire and do all we can to transform ourselves and the world around us.

XII

The art of creativity is the essence of simplicity
Conveyed with authenticity and skill
Whatever our medium and message
We all have a role to fulfil
If we're to move beyond our safe limitations
And redeem who we truly are
We need to trust ourselves and each other
And be determined to follow our star

Trusting our dream, our inner vision, prompting or calling, takes great faith, courage and self-belief. Yet where would we be without the dreamers of this world?…

By aligning mind, heart, body and soul to what we know is true, we connect to our guiding light within that shows us the way.

Dare to listen to what your soul is calling you to do and be.

XIII

We all have infinite potential
Is our brain lying half asleep?
Imagine if everyone here and now
Made a promise to dig down deep
And every day on awakening
Chose not to stay the same
But to realise their unique potential
Which bears their very own name

There is always something we can do, or stop doing, to raise our game, transform ourselves and make the world a brighter place.

If you are unsure where your gifts and potential lie, ask people who know you well and will tell you the truth. You are unique and have something special to offer. Where do you find joy? What makes your heart sing? What do other people love most about you? Asking these questions, and exploring the answers, with a family member or friend as support, could help signpost you to an exciting new hobby, job, or rewarding voluntary work.

XIV

The art of creativity is heightened sensitivity
Connection to our purpose and our power
When our energy has dwindled
We can choose to be rekindled,
Life is the Tao of the now
Dare to open the door, let your inner fire roar
Let your passion like a beacon burn bright
May your imagination, light up our constellation
Blaze a trail across the indigo night!

Just like the Phoenix, we can choose to be rekindled. The call is to meet our trials with creative fire.

The more each one of us opens up to our innate, creative spirit and expresses our passion and joy, the more we will rise and move beyond our personal and collective challenges.

We are One.

Be a Keeper of the Flame.

Part Two

The Ascent of the Phoenix

The Ascent of the Phoenix
— *rising above and beyond*

The Ascent of the Phoenix is a creative, interactive project built around a Ten-point Call to Action.

The Intention

To kindle around the world:

> Connection
>
> Communication
>
> Collaboration

The Vision

To inspire the creation of a *Phoenix Imaginarium* — a resource of creative work that uplifts the spirit and feeds the soul. Imagine if we pooled our ideas and original creativity inspired by the risen vision of the Phoenix. This would help to focus our mind and heart on innovation and new beginnings to support the raising of global consciousness.

The Invitation

You are warmly invited to help manifest the *Phoenix Imaginarium* by engaging in three or more activities from the Ten-point Call to Action. The ideas explore a wide range of tastes. This gives you the opportunity of trying out new things like responding with your own original creativity or choosing your own film, song, music video, poem or quotations inspired by the symbol of the Phoenix.

Purpose

To inspire personal and collective transformation

Aims

- To ignite the creative spirit
- To unleash the power of imagination
- To spark a sense of play, fun and joy
- To celebrate the Phoenix as a symbol of regeneration

Mantra

> Every day, in every way, I'm getting lighter and lighter.

The Ascent of the Phoenix Mantra takes its inspiration, word format and suggested practice, from the tried and tested method of 'Conscious Autosuggestion' pioneered by French psychologist and pharmacist Émile Coué de la Châtaigneraie (1857-1926).

Coué maintained that curing some of our troubles requires a change in our unconscious thought, which can be achieved only by using our imagination. His popular method of psychotherapy and self-improvement was based on the following autosuggestion which he recommended be used at the beginning and at the end of each day when the unconscious mind is particularly receptive.

"Every day, in every way, I'm getting better and better."
(French: "*Tous les jours à tous points de vue je vais de mieux en mieux.*")

Couéism was further spread into popular culture in the '80s through the lyrics of the well-known pop song by John Lennon, 'Beautiful Boy', which he wrote for his son, Sean. Lennon referenced the Coué method in the chorus.

The Ten-point Call to Action

Choose three ideas from the following, or more if you wish. Explore them on your own or create an Ascent of the Phoenix hub of two or more to experiment, discuss and share.

The model set out below incorporates my choice of personal favourites. Nos. 3-6 are a way of exemplifying the creative idea and igniting the initial flame. I can't wait to hear what your choices are and to see them circulating on social media.

1. Say the Mantra at least two or three times a day and preferably first thing in the morning and last thing at night by reciting or affirming inwardly.

    Every day, in every way, I'm getting lighter and lighter.

2. Respond to the theme The Ascent of the Phoenix using any creative medium that inspires you.

3. Watch and share a television programme, Youtube clip or film based on an inspirational story about following your passion, such as:

    Eddie the Eagle – a 2016 British biographical sports comedy-drama film starring Taron Egerton as Michael Edwards, a British skier who in 1988 became the first competitor to represent Great Britain in Olympic ski jumping since 1928.

4. Choose an uplifting piece of music, song or music video that resonates with the symbol of the Phoenix. Watch and listen to this beautiful lyric video on Youtube.

    'I am Light' by India Arie

5. Find an inspirational poem about regeneration and resilience or write your own. Savour the charismatic Maya Angelou reciting her poem on Youtube.

    'Still I Rise'

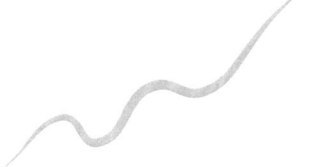

6. Find a quotation that delights or provides soul food,

> "Give light and people will find the way."   Ella Baker

7. Recite 'The Circle of Peace Dedication' to raise your spirits and send peaceful thoughts out to the world. Set the words to music of your own or download the choral arrangement (it's free) by going to the Get Involved page on <u>www.theglobalcircleofpeace.com</u>

> Peace in every home and heart
> Peace across our land
> Peace in every mind and body
> Peace in every hand

8. Reflect on and share the Verses and Reflections in Part I of this book. Write down or sketch insights or observations that come to mind.

9. Contemplate the following burning question:

    How much is enough?

    Write down your findings and share with your family, a friend or your community group.

10. Arrange an Ascent of the Phoenix casual social gathering – online or in real time – to share your insights, discoveries and creative ideas Celebrate the Phoenix and share your photos and experiences with others.

You have been handed a torch. Please keep the creative fire of the Phoenix alive.

What To Do Next

We would love to hear from you with your creative response to The Ascent of the Phoenix Ten-point Call to Action.

Do send in your original work and inspired personal choices, the more we circulate all the ideas the better. You can either send your contribution as an email with the header *Phoenix Imaginarium* or go to the Blog Submissions page on the website. Any original work you send in will remain your copyright and be attributed to you.

To learn more about *PhoenixWisdom*, I warmly invite you to visit my website and book a free fifteen-minute consultation by filling out the form on the Contact Page.

    email: <u>info@flythephoenix.co.uk</u>
    www.facebook.com/FlythePhoenix
    Twitter:@flythephoenix
    Instagram: flythephoenixnow
    <u>www.flythephoenix.co.uk</u>

"Man is the centre of a circle without a circumference, except the one he creates for himself."

— *Mahatma Gandhi*